P9-DGS-742

DOEDICURUS

PREHISTORIC BEASTS
DOEDICURUS

MARC ZABLUDOFF
ILLUSTRATED BY PETER BOLLINGER

Marshall Cavendish
Benchmark

New York

Published by Marshall Cavendish Benchmark
An imprint of Marshall Cavendish Corporation

Website: www.marshallcavendish.us

This publication represents the opinions and views of the author based on Marc Zabludoff's personal experience, knowledge, and research. The information in this book serves as a general guide only. The author and publisher have used their best efforts in preparing this book and disclaim liability rising directly and indirectly from the use and application of this book.

Other Marshall Cavendish Offices: Marshall Cavendish International (Asia) Private Limited, 1 New Industrial Road, Singapore 536196 • Marshall Cavendish International (Thailand) Co Ltd. 253 Asoke, 12th Flr, Sukhumvit 21 Road, Klongtoey Nua, Wattana, Bangkok 10110, Thailand • Marshall Cavendish (Malaysia) Sdn Bhd, Times Subang, Lot 46, Subang Hi-Tech Industrial Park, Batu Tiga, 40000 Shah Alam, Selangor Darul Ehsan, Malaysia

Marshall Cavendish is a trademark of Times Publishing Limited

All websites were available and accurate when this book was sent to press.

Library of Congress Cataloging-in-Publication Data
Zabludoff, Marc.
Doedicurus / Marc Zabludoff ; illustrated by Peter Bollinger.
p. cm.—(Prehistoric beasts)
Summary: "Explore Doedicurus, its physical characteristics, when and where it lived, how it lived, what other animals lived alongside it, and how we know this"—Provided by publisher.
Includes bibliographical references and index.
ISBN 978-1-60870-033-2
1. Doedicurus—Juvenile literature. I. Bollinger, Peter, ill. II. Title.
QE882.E2Z33 2011
569'.31--dc22
2009044589

Editor: Christine Florie
Publisher: Michelle Bisson
Art Director: Anahid Hamparian
Series Designer: Alicia Mikles

Photo research by Connie Gardner

The photographs in this book are used by permission and through the courtesy of:
Corbis: Robert Kerian, 11 (B); *Superstock:* Tom Murphy, 15.

Printed in Malaysia (T)
1 3 5 6 4 2

CONTENTS

AT HOME IN SOUTH AMERICA

On this midsummer day the sky is a brilliant blue, and the fields are buzzing with insects. Thousands of miles to the north, in a land that, 30,000 years from now, will be called Canada, a mile-thick slab of ice covers the ground. But here, on the plains of the future Argentina, in South America, the land is green, carpeted with tall stalks of grass that wave gently in the breeze.

Something is munching its way slowly through the grass—something large. From a distance it looks like one of the giant tortoises that inhabit the islands far to the northwest, in the Pacific Ocean. But it is much bigger than a tortoise and much stranger. It has not just a large, rounded shell but also a kind of helmet atop a furry head. Its tail, though, is not furry at all. It seems to be made of hard rings, and at its end are vicious spikes.

The animal is a female, for there is a smaller animal nuzzling under the shell to grab a quick meal of milk. While the mother walks, the youngster

Doedicurus's **natural habitat was the plains, where lush grasses thrived and provided the animal with a bounty of food.**

7

waddles by her side. It is easy to trace the path they have traveled. The big animal's tail swishes widely as she walks, flattening the uneaten grass behind her on either side.

Other than the sounds of her chewing and the buzz of the insects, the scene is quiet. Then a deep roar rolls across the plain—the threatening call of a lion-size cat. Although the grass eater cannot see the cat, she can tell it is not far away. Still, she shows no concern, other than to make sure her youngster is by her side. There is no need for her to stop eating.

Someday a human will give this strange animal the name *Doedicurus* (dee-dik-YOO-russ). By then, however, the great beast will be long gone from the world.

TANKS ON THE PRAIRIE

Although *Doedicurus* was a mammal, it lived inside a suit of armor like a giant tortoise—a **reptile**—would. Like all mammals, *Doedicurus* had fur or hair, but little of it showed. Its hard shell, called a **carapace**, covered its entire back and sides. When not moving, *Doedicurus* must have looked like a boulder sitting in a field.

This ancient animal's armor was as much as 2 inches thick and made of nearly two thousand small, six-sided bone plates that were cemented together. When joined, they formed a dome that rose over the animal's back. The dome was not completely solid—it was pierced with small holes through which thin clumps of hair probably grew.

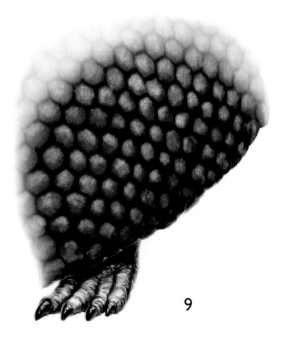

Doedicurus's domed shell was made of about two thousand hard plates. It helped protect the animal from the teeth of predators.

9

But the bony shell was rigid. It did not bend at all, except along the edges. There *Doedicurus*'s armor was a bit more flexible, and when the beast walked it flowed like a stiff, protective skirt over its legs.

On top of *Doedicurus*'s head was a separate cap of bone. The cap did not cover the entire face, and fur peeked out along the snout. *Doedicurus*'s tail, though, was completely surrounded by bone in the shape of rings. The rings allowed the tail to swing back and forth. When the tail moved, anything in its path was in danger. At the end of this tail was a large knob adorned with big, hornlike spikes.

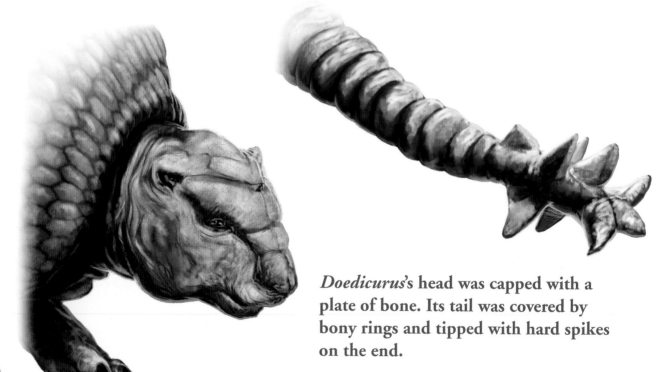

***Doedicurus*'s head was capped with a plate of bone. Its tail was covered by bony rings and tipped with hard spikes on the end.**

An adult _Doedicurus_ was as long as a modern car.

WHAT DOES THE NAME _DOEDICURUS_ MEAN?

Doedicurus means "pestle tail." When scientists first saw the fossilized tail bones, the bones lacked their horny spikes. The discoverers thought the large, rounded bone at the end of the tail looked like a pestle, a knob-shaped tool used for grinding spices, herbs, or chemicals.

As an adult _Doedicurus_ was about the size of a car, stretching as much as 13 feet from the tip of its nose to the tip of its tail. The top of its carapace was 5.5 feet above the ground. Underneath the armor was a massive body weighing 2,000 to 3,000 pounds, held up by four thick, short legs. Each leg ended in a four-toed foot. Each toe was capped with a blunt claw that was almost like a hoof.

11

For such a large animal, *Doedicurus*'s head was rather small from front to back. But it was big from top to bottom. The head was made huge by *Doedicurus*'s powerful jaws, which housed a set of large, blocky grinding teeth on the sides of the mouth. *Doedicurus* had no biting teeth in front. Like a rhinoceros, it probably had strong lips for pulling in its meals of grass, tough plants, and perhaps roots that it dug up with its heavy claws.

EVOLUTION OF AN ODD MAMMAL

Where did such a beast come from, and what made it look so strange? The short answer to both questions is South America.

Although the two continents of North and South America share a name, for nearly 60 million years they were unconnected. Central America did not yet exist, and South America was a gigantic island, cut off from all the other continents by oceans. For the most part, animals living in South America were unable to mix with animals living anywhere else. As a result, they sometimes **evolved** in unusual ways.

Among the oddest of South American animals were a group of mammals called the **xenarthrans**. The only animals from that group still living today are armadillos, tree sloths, and anteaters. Once upon a time, though, there were many more members, including giant, 10,000-pound ground sloths and a collection of armored plant eaters called **glyptodonts**.

The earliest glyptodonts were medium-size animals with thin and

probably flexible armor, like their modern cousins, the armadillos. As the centuries passed, however, glyptodonts grew bigger, and their armor grew thicker and more rigid. After tens of millions of years the glyptodont group included the tanklike *Doedicurus*.

The armadillo is a cousin of early glyptodonts. How many similarities with *Doedicurus* can you find?

Doedicurus was well protected against **predators**—and it needed to be. By the time it first appeared, a little less than 2 million years ago, Central America had formed a link between North and South America. For the first time animals were able to walk from one continent to the other. Among those wandering south were large plant eaters, such as the elephant-like **mastodons**. But along with them came meat eaters such as jaguars and fierce **saber-toothed cats**. A peaceful vegetarian might have found some extra protection quite useful.

◀ *Doedicurus* **shared its home with giant ground sloths.**

DID YOU KNOW?

When North and South America joined, some familiar animals moved into their present homes for the first time. Some of the animals that traveled north were porcupines and opossums. Among the animals that traveled south were llamas.

MYSTERIOUS EVIDENCE

Except for the fact that *Doedicurus* ate grass—and that it must have spent much of its time eating—there is little that scientists can say for certain about how *Doedicurus* lived.

Paleontologists can sometimes make only their best guess as to how an **extinct** animal behaved. Often, the only hard facts they have are the **fossil** bones the animal left behind. But the story the bones tell is not always clear.

For instance, *Doedicurus*'s spiked tail certainly appears to be a weapon to use against an enemy. More than anything else, it resembles a mace—a spiked club swung by a medieval knight in armor centuries ago. Swinging low to the ground, *Doedicurus*'s mighty club would have crushed the bones of any meat eater it met.

However, *Doedicurus* was probably a clumsy warrior. Because of its

◀ **Scientists are certain that *Doedicurus* ate a lot. But they cannot say much more about its behavior.**

armor, the mighty beast could not see well to the sides or rear. It also could not move very fast. Not only was *Doedicurus* very heavy and its legs short, but its carapace was attached to its hip bones. This limited its movements. Finally, although we can say that *Doedicurus*'s tail *could* have broken a predator's bones, we have no fossil legs or skulls that we can definitively say were broken by such a weapon.

JUST HOW POWERFUL WAS *DOEDICURUS*'S TAIL?

The bony tail was about 4 feet long, weighed 90 pounds, and was very muscular. A swinging *Doedicurus* tail would have been like a chain of five or six heavy bowling balls flying through the air at high speed.

Doedicurus **might have used its tail to fight off predators like this terror bird.**

LIFESTYLES OF THE BIG AND BONY

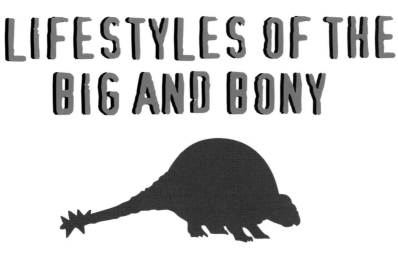

Paleontologists do have other bones, though, that show exactly the kind of damage *Doedicurus*'s tail could have caused. But these fossils do not come from the great beast's predators. They are the dented and crushed bony carapaces of *Doedicurus* itself.

Doedicurus probably used its club to fight with others of its own kind. Most likely, the fighters were males. The winner of the battle would get territory or a female *Doedicurus* as his prize. Determining precisely how one *Doedicurus* fought another calls for some imagination. Perhaps the two simply stood side by side, smashing each other with their tails again and again until one of them finally gave up.

Today, many male animals use their "weapons" to fight other males

Doedicurus **males probably used their heavy, spiked tails to strike other males in fights over mates and territory.**

over mates. Male deer, for example, battle each other with their antlers. So *Doedicurus* using its tail for that same purpose makes sense. Besides, it does not seem likely that *Doedicurus* actually needed its frightening tail much for defense. Even if a hungry saber-toothed cat somehow managed to kill a *Doedicurus*, it would have had a hard time turning the beast over to get at any of the soft parts. *Doedicurus* did not need a heavy, spiked tail to protect itself.

DID YOU KNOW?

Doedicurus was among the most well-protected mammals ever to walk on Earth. The only other animal built like it was not a mammal but a dinosaur, named *Ankylosaurus*. It too had heavy armor covering its body and head and a club at the end of its tail. But it vanished more than 60 million years before *Doedicurus* appeared.

Still, *Doedicurus* might have used its tail to protect its babies. A young *Doedicurus* was small enough for a predator to handle, and its shell was probably thin enough to bite through. In fact, there are young glyptodont skulls showing the kind of injuries that would have been made by a large cat's long teeth.

Doedicurus was too big an animal to have hidden its baby in a den or in a nest, as armadillos do. Most likely, it guarded its youngsters until they grew large enough to watch out for themselves. Just how it protected its offspring we can never really know. But it is not difficult to imagine a mother or even a pair of armored giants shielding a youngster with their front ends while their deadly tails swung blindly, clearing the ground of any predators.

A TANKLESS WORLD

Doedicurus lived on Earth until around ten thousand years ago. Then it disappeared forever, at the end of the great Ice Age. That ice age was only the last in a long series of cold periods that had been coming and going for nearly 2 million years. Overall, they made our planet a rather different place from what it had once been.

During the Ice Age, winters were not much colder than they are now. But summers were cool enough that the snow and ice never melted. The oceans, without melting ice to refill them, became lower. Less rain fell. Forests shrank. Prairies grew.

This changed Earth was one that suited *Doedicurus*. Its South American home was never covered with ice, as much of North America was. But the cooler, drier climate produced huge areas of grasslands and woods in which the big animal thrived.

It is not known why and how *Doedicurus* became extinct, but one factor may have been the changing climate of its natural habitat.

Exactly why it went extinct is a mystery. As the planet warmed and the ice finally melted, many of Earth's largest animals disappeared. Among them were the **mammoths** and the mastodons, the saber-toothed cats, the giant ground sloths, and all the glyptodonts.

Some scientists think humans are at least partly to blame. As the Ice Age ended, humans arrived in the Americas for the first time. They brought with them new, stone-tipped weapons, and it is possible that they hunted some large animals to extinction.

Is it likely, though, that people alone killed off *Doedicurus*? Surely early hunters found animals that were easier to kill and cook than a 3,000-pound, club-tailed tank.

Quite possibly it was a changing world that doomed *Doedicurus*. The end of the Ice Age was a time of rapid changes in Earth's climate and in the kinds of plants that grew across South America. Perhaps the animal's food supplies shrank dangerously. Perhaps *Doedicurus* simply faced too much competition from other grass eaters. Whatever the exact cause, Earth became a place where even a tank of a mammal could no longer survive.

TIMELINE

65 million years ago	Dinosaurs become extinct.
60 million years ago	Armadillo and glyptodont ancestors evolve on the isolated continent of South America.
3 million years ago	South America joins with North America via Central America; animals start to move between continents.
2.5 million years ago	Earth's climate begins to cool; grasslands spread throughout South America.
1.8 million years ago	An ice age begins; *Doedicurus* appears in South America.
100,000 years ago	The last Ice Age begins.
20,000 years ago	The great Ice Age peaks; huge ice sheets cover North America as far south as Wisconsin.
15,000 years ago	Earth begins to warm.
12,000 years ago	Ice sheets begin to melt; major ecological changes take place in the Northern Hemisphere; humans arrive in Alaska.
10,000 years ago	The great Ice Age ends; *Doedicurus* and other large Ice Age mammals become extinct.

27

GLOSSARY

carapace (kar-uh-peys) hard outer covering of an animal, such as the shell of a turtle.

evolve to change over many thousands and millions of years.

extinct gone forever.

fossil preserved remains of an animal or plant.

glyptodont (GLIP-tuh-don't) group of extinct mammals, related to modern armadillos, that had hard outer shells made of bone.

mammoth extinct, hairy member of the elephant family.

mastodon extinct member of the elephant family that was common in the Americas.

paleontologist scientist who studies fossils to learn about life in the past.

predator animal that hunts and eats other animals.

reptile one of the group of egg-laying animals that includes lizards and turtles.

saber-toothed cat an extinct Ice Age meat eater that had two long, pointed teeth.

xenarthran (ze-NAR-thren) one of the group of mammals that includes all sloths, anteaters, armadillos, and the extinct glyptodonts.

FIND OUT MORE

Book

Zabludoff, Marc. *Giant Ground Sloth*. New York: Marshall Cavendish Benchmark, 2010.

DVD

Walking with Prehistoric Beasts. BBC/Warner Home Video, 2002.

Websites

The Life of Mammals

www.bbc.co.uk/nature/animals/mammals/challenges/

"Mammal Maker Game" and "Beast Feast" are two interactive games on the BBC Science & Nature site that allow users to explore the range of mammals' body types and diets.

Walking with Beasts

www.abc.net.au/beasts/factfiles/

This site contains facts about and illustrations of more than thirty prehistoric animals, including *Doedicurus*.

Giant Armadillo

www.arkive.org/species/GES/mammals/Priodontes_maximus/

www.kidsplanet.org/factsheets/armadillo.html

Among *Doedicurus*'s closest living relatives is the giant armadillo—one-thirtieth the weight of its extinct cousin, but a true giant among its kin.

INDEX

Page numbers in **boldface** are illustrations.

ABOUT THE AUTHOR

Marc Zabludoff, the former editor in chief of *Discover* magazine, has been involved in communicating science to the public for more than two decades. His other work for Marshall Cavendish includes books on spiders, beetles, and monkeys for the AnimalWays series, along with books on insects, reptiles, and the largely unknown and chiefly microscopic organisms known as protoctists. Zabludoff lives in New York City with his wife and daughter.

ABOUT THE ILLUSTRATOR

Peter Bollinger is an award-winning illustrator whose clients include those in the publishing, advertising, and entertainment industries. Bollinger works in two separate styles, traditional airbrush and digital illustration. He lives in California with his wife, son, and daughter.